Melbourne
& Victoria's Splendour

NEW HOLLAND

INTRODUCTION

Tucked below the Murray River in south-eastern Australia, Victoria may be the second-smallest state in the nation but it has the second-largest population, with two-thirds of Victorians living in Melbourne — the state's sophisticated and cosmopolitan coastal capital and Australia's second-largest city. Outside Melbourne, and all within easy driving distance, Victoria is dotted with towns large and small, from the isolated villages of the rugged eastern highlands to the agricultural centres of the Murray basin in the north-west and the fishing ports found along the length of the state's spectacular and varied coastline.

First settled by the British in response to fears of rival occupation by the French — and in spite of Aboriginal resistance — the area now known as Victoria became a separate colony from New South Wales in 1851, just as the Australian gold-rushes began. As people flocked to the goldfields around Ballarat and Bendigo, the colony's population soared in less than a year from a little under 100,000 to over half a million.

Much of the wealth engendered was poured into the many fine buildings, public and private, still in evidence throughout Victoria today — magnificent edifices such as Ballarat's imposing Town Hall, completed in the 1870s, Bendigo's splendidly decorated Italianate Shamrock Hotel, and the many well-preserved historic buildings which contribute to the unique architectural fabric of modern Melbourne. St Patrick's Cathedral is a spectacular example of Gothic Revival architecture with a spire soaring 100 metres above the street, and the vast bluestone and freestone bulk of Parliament House, with its sweeping steps and grand colonnade, presides over the city centre from the top of Bourke Street.

But Melbourne today is more than magnificent buildings — Australia's vibrant cultural capital of over 3.1 million people wrapped around the Yarra River offers a smorgasbord of diverse experiences. City life reflects the well-known Melburnian loves of culture, coffee and sport — not necessarily in that order. While the city (in fact the whole state!) takes a public holiday for the Melbourne Cup held at Flemington racecourse each November, the Victorian Arts Centre in the arts precinct near the Princes Bridge is home to the Australian Ballet. And the multitude of theatres and festivals — including the world-class International Comedy Festival and the Melbourne International Festival of the Arts — combine to cement Melbourne's reputation as Australia's centre for the performing arts.

Above: Intricate decorations adorn a Melbourne lamppost.

If you prefer retail therapy to the National Gallery, and the amazing sculptures along the promenade at the Southgate complex are the closest you get to art, why not shop 'til you drop at Melbourne Central, Australia's largest retail shopping complex. Or take a tram to the bustling Queen Victoria Markets, where hundreds of stalls offer everything from seafood to handicrafts, before you head for cafe hotspots across the city like seaside St Kilda, Brunswick Street, Fitzroy, and Chapel Street, Prahran.

Melbourne is not all hustle — the Royal Botanic, Alexandra and Queen Victoria gardens stretch invitingly alongside the Yarra, providing tranquil relief from the buzz, and for those who yearn for more wide open spaces, much of the rest of the state is within easy reach of the city. The rolling Dandenong Ranges rise just to the east, Little Penguins march nightly across the beach at Phillip Island to the south, and the spectacular rock formations visible from the Great Ocean Road west of the city are only a short drive away. A bit further afield, rugged Wilsons Promontory — the southernmost point of the Australian mainland — juts into Bass Strait, and the snowfields in the high country lie only a few hours to the north-east. With so much to see and so much to explore, this book presents you with the tip of the iceberg of Melbourne and Victoria's splendours.

Left: Brightly coloured bathing boxes line Brighton Beach in Melbourne.

Above: Melbourne's stately trams add living transport history to the city's ambience.

Left: Once the busiest station in the world, the neo-classical edifice of Flinders Street Station has been a favourite city landmark since its completion in 1910.

Previous pages: As dusk falls over Melbourne the lights of the city reflect beautifully in the bay.

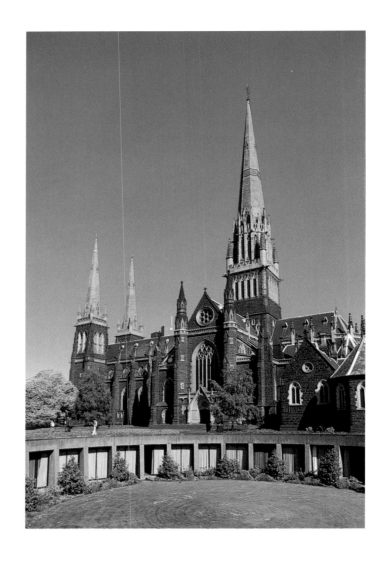

Above left: Fine mosaics, carving and magnificent stained glass are hidden within the gothic-style edifice of St Paul's Anglican Cathedral. It was opened for worship in 1891 with the spires finally completed in 1933.

Above right: St Patrick's Cathedral, completed in 1897, is another splendid example of Gothic Revival architecture.

Opposite: The imposing freestone face of Parliament House stares across the city from the top of Bourke Street.

12   Above: The gracious colonial mansion of 'Como' in South Yarra is an unusual mix of Australian Regency and Italianate styles of architecture.

Above: Cloaked in grey granite, the Shrine of Remembrance in parkland near St Kilda Road commemorates Victorians who served in World War I.   13

Above: The lights on the Westgate Bridge across the Yarra twinkle as dusk falls over the city.

Left: Early morning sun makes the buildings of the city glow with a golden light.

Above: The Victorian Arts Centre, home to the Australian Ballet, is Australia's largest cultural centre.

Right: Theatres abound in Melbourne and the Princess Theatre in Spring Street, complete with flying cherubs, dome and ornate plasterwork, is one of the finest.

Above and top: Regarded as Australia's cultural capital, Melbourne is also home
to the Australian Ballet and the Melbourne Symphony Orchestra.

Left: Thousands gather for open air concerts at the spectacular Sidney Myer Music Bowl.

20   Above: Melbourne is a festival city — there's Moomba in March then Comedy, Film, Writers' and International Arts festivals later in the year.

Above: Melbourne's Aquarium offers a fascinating glimpse of the ocean's realm.

Above: Melbourne Central in the heart of the city is Australia's largest retail complex with shopping galore.

Right: The shops of Melbourne cater for all tastes and budgets — visit the 'Paris' end of Collins Street for a touch of class.

Above: A Swanston Street flower stall adds a splash of colour to the streetscape of the city.

Left: Children and adults alike are entranced by enchanting Christmas displays.

Above: Lively Queen Victoria Market, just a few streets from the city centre, has hundreds of stalls offering everything from fresh fruit and vegetables to seafood, leathergoods and pets.

Right: A brightly coloured mural enlivens the bustle of the marketplace.

Above: The Fairy Tree in Fitzroy Gardens was carved by Olna Cohn between 1931 and 1934.

Left: Cooks' Cottage, the home of Captain James Cook's parents, was built in 1755 in Great Ayton, England, transported to Australia in 1933 and presented to the State of Victoria in 1934.

Following pages: Melbourne's magnificent Queen Victoria Gardens date from the early 1900s.

Above left: Many marvellous sculptures stand in and around the Conservatory
in the beautiful Fitzroy Gardens behind Parliament House.

Above right: Melbourne's Queen Victoria Gardens are strewn with wonderful works of art.

Right: Spreading over 35 hectares beside the Yarra River, Melbourne's Royal Botanic Gardens
— constructed in the 19th century landscape tradition — rank amongst the top
botanical gardens in the world.

Above: Wonderful sculptures adorn Southgate — the complex of shops, restaurants and cafes beside the Arts Centre on the banks of the Yarra.

Right: Deborah Halpern's monumentally marvellous sculpture 'Angel' emerges from the pool outside the National Gallery of Victoria.

Above: A futuristic footbridge arches over the Yarra in front of the Southgate Complex and Southbank.

Opposite: Fireworks burst over Melbourne's Crown Casino, part of the Crown Entertainment Complex which houses fourteen 24-hour cinemas and thirty restaurants as well as nightclubs and luxury shops.

Above: A double scull slips through tranquil waters in the last of the fading light.

Right: Rowers gather under bright blue skies at the boatshed slips on the Yarra River.

Above and top: If there's one thing Melburnians like more than their football it's a great cricket match at the famous Melbourne Cricket Ground.

Left: The frocks are out and the hats are on as Australia comes to a complete halt once a year for the Melbourne Cup at Flemington racecourse.

Following pages: Eager tennis fans pack Court One for the Australian Open at Melbourne Park.

Above and top: The once working-class suburb of Carlton, like inner-city suburbs across Australia, is undergoing a yuppie renovation invasion.

Left: Chapel Street in South Yarra is just one of many cafe hotspots across Melbourne.

Above and right: Flower shops, galleries, cafes, restaurants and bars — busy Brunswick Street in Fitzroy has something for everyone.

Following pages: The bright lights of Brunswick Street attract revellers from across the city.

Above: Crowds have been flocking to St Kilda's Luna Park — an old-fashioned seaside funfair full of fairy floss and ferris wheels — since 1901.

Above: Rollerbladers take advantage of glorious sunshine and blue skies on St Kilda's seemingly endless pier.

Above left and right: Brightly coloured sculptures adorn rooftops along St Kilda's streets.

Left: Acland Street in St Kilda is famous for its enticing range of continental cake shops.

Following pages: Melbourne's city skyline rises above boats moored off Williamstown.

Above: Pleasure boats crowd the marina at the Brighton Yacht Club just south of St Kilda in Melbourne.

Above: Crescents of golden sand and clear blue waters make Brighton seem far away from Melbourne's CBD.

Above: A ride on the Puffing Billy steam train from Belgrave to Emerald Creek is an exciting way
to explore the ferny forest gullies of the Dandenong Ranges.

Opposite: Autumn leaves carpet the water near the picturesque boathouse at the Alfred Nicholas Gardens in the Dandenongs.

Previous pages: Brightly coloured bathing huts lining the beach at Brighton conjure up images of earlier times.

Above: Tesselaar's annual Tulip Festival at Silvan in the Dandenongs is a feast for the eyes.

Left: Towering mountain ash, replanted after the devastating Black Friday bushfires of January 1939, soar skywards in the Black Spur forest near Healesville.

Above: Koalas clamber contentedly around the gum trees of the Healesville Sanctuary.

Right: Selovers lookout near Healesville offers a picturesque view over Maroondah Reservoir — the source of much of Melbourne's water.

Above: Healesville has been a summer resort for Melburnians since the turn of the century.

Left: A farmer tends vines on the Tarraford Estate near Yarra Glen just north of Melbourne.

Following pages: Known as Yarra Flats until 1889, Yarra Glen is surrounded
by lush agricultural and dairy lands.

Above: Little Penguins parade across the beach each evening on Phillip Island south of Melbourne.

Top: The Penguin Parade Visitor Centre just behind the beach is filled with penguin information.

Left: A long boardwalk leads to an excellent vantage point over the Nobbies rock formation.

Above: The Nobbies at dusk seem like creatures from the deep, the blowhole nearby breathing with the surge of the sea.

Opposite: It's not hard to see why this spot on Phillip Island is called Red Rocks.

Following pages: Giant boulders dwarf trees at Squeaky Beach on Wilsons Promontory, the mainland's southernmost point.

Above: Nets litter the jetty at Lakes Entrance, the home port of Australia's largest fishing fleet.

Right: Visitors to Lakes Entrance can choose from boating and windsurfing on the lakes,
a frolic in the surf at Ninety Mile Beach or the tranquil beauty of a sunset stroll
down by the jetties.

Above: The Bairnsdale courthouse, finished in 1893, boasts gables, towers and a cedar interior.

Top: Broad verandahs with intricate ironwork surround Bairnsdale's Grand Terminus Hotel.

Left: The pretty swing bridge across the Latrobe River near Sale was built in 1883 to allow steamers and barges to pass through to Melbourne.

Above: Wind whips along the dunes between Ninety Mile Beach and the tiny town of Seaspray.

Right: Within the Croajingolong National Park lie the tranquil waters of the Malacoota Inlet.

Above: A surfer makes his way back to the spectator area at a Bells Beach surfing competition.

Top: Surfers settle for less at Lorne, a charming beachside town with many old-style guesthouses.

Left: The beach at Torquay doesn't beat Bells but the town is a mecca for surfers.

Following pages: The crane at the end of the jetty at Lorne lifts vessels to safety during storms.

Above: The lonely Cape Otway lighthouse offers panoramic views along the coast.

Right: A crayfishing boat rests beside the jetty at Apollo Bay, once a thriving timber port.

Following pages: The mainland arch of the spectacular London Bridge rock formation collapsed suddenly in 1990, stranding visitors unharmed on the remaining outcrop.

Above: The spectacular Twelve Apostles (in fact there are only eight) are hardy remnants of an earlier mainland cliff front.

Opposite: The beauty of the Loch Ard Gorge belies its tragic history — the *Loch Ard* sank nearby with only two survivors.

Above: The Great Ocean Road stretches for 320 kilometres from Anglesea to Peterborough — hugging the clifftops here, dipping down to beaches there, and soaring over the Otway Ranges.

Opposite: Tessellations seem to shatter the rock platform at Wye River near Apollo Bay along the Great Ocean Road.

Following pages: Picturesque Port Fairy on the Moyne River was one of the busiest shipping ports in Australia in the 1850s.

Above: The Eureka flag was first raised over the Eureka Stockade in Ballarat during an 1854 armed insurrection by aggrieved gold miners who briefly proclaimed a 'Republic of Victoria'.

Left: Bentley's Hotel 'burns' in the Eureka Stockade Centre's nightly 'Blood on the Southern Cross' — a sound and light show telling the story of the Eureka uprising.

Above: Brightly coloured begonias are lovingly tended in preparation for the annual Begonia Festival in Ballarat's botanical gardens.

Right: Ballarat's Town Hall, a mighty Victorian edifice built during the 1860s and 70s, replaced the original weatherboard structure built five years after the discovery of gold in 1851.

Above: It is possible to strike it lucky panning for gold in Red Hill Creek at the Sovereign Hill Historical Park at Ballarat. Thousands of dollars in real gold are deposited every year for you to find.

Left: The Sovereign Hill 'living museum' recreates a prosperous 1850s goldmining township.

Above left and above right: The Alexandra Fountain glows at dusk in Bendigo
— once a rich goldmining centre, it is now Victoria's fourth-largest city.

Opposite: Built on gold money in 1897, the highly decorated Italianate Shamrock Hotel in Bendigo was one of the finest
buildings of its time, with hot and cold running water and electric lights and bells in every room.

Above: The pretty mountain township of Daylesford, known during the goldrush as Jim Crow Diggings,
is now a popular tourist destination famed for its mineral springs.

Opposite: The market centre of Castlemaine serves a productive dairying and sheep-grazing region south of Bendigo.

Following pages: Just a short drive from Mount Macedon, Hanging Rock — of the book and the film *Picnic at Hanging Rock* — rises 120 metres to provide sweeping views across the surrounding rolling hills.

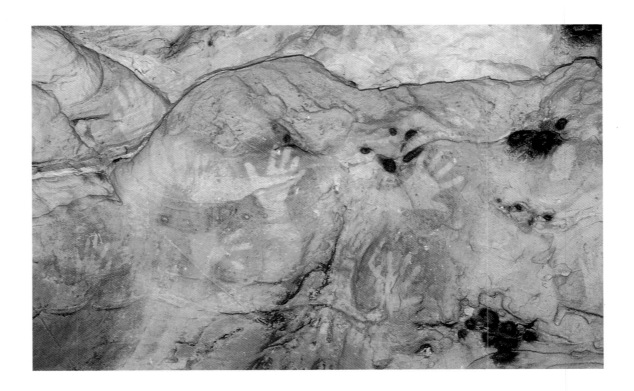

Above: Aboriginal hand stencils cover the walls of the Manja shelter on the Harrop Track.

Left: Hard metamorphic rock makes a water sculpture of the falls on the MacKenzie River.

Following pages: The Balconies rock formation provides a magnificent view
across the Grampians (Gariwerd) National Park.

Grampians

Above: Mount Abrupt rises behind cow-covered farmland at the southern end of the park.

Right: Leaves glow in the sun at Halls Gap, named after a pastoralist who followed the route taken by Aborigines across the mountains.

Above: A freestyle skier floats through the air at Mount Buller, Victoria's largest ski resort.

Left: What view? A rockclimber pauses on 'Peroxide Blond' — a climb on the face of The Horn, the highest peak in Mount Buffalo National Park.

Following pages: Mount Feathertop and Razorback Ridge catch the afternoon light.

Above: A mountain stream flows through Centenary Park in the tiny highland town of Bright.

Right: Magnificent autumn colours draw thousands of visitors to Bright every year.

Above: Freshly picked sultana grapes dry on racks in the sun on a farm not far from Mildura on the Murray River.

Left: Table grapes are protected from the weather near Mildura in the heart of the Sunraysia irrigation area, known for its vine and citrus fruit production.

Above: Step back in time at Swan Hill's National Trust-classified 1840s homestead 'Tyntynder'.

Right: A bridge over the Murray at Swan Hill is a reminder that the town began as a river crossing point in 1846 and developed as a river port in the days of the paddle-wheelers.

Above: A booming Murray River port until the advent of the railways, Echuca was first reached by paddle steamer in 1853.

Above: Gums along the banks of the Murray River near Robinvale glow golden in the early morning light.

Published in Australia by
New Holland Publishers (Australia) Pty Ltd
Sydney • Auckland • London • Cape Town
14 Aquatic Drive Frenchs Forest NSW 2086 Australia
278 Lake Road Northcote Auckland New Zealand
24 Nutford Place London W1H 5DQ United Kingdom
80 McKenzie Street Cape Town 8001 South Africa

First published in 1998 and reprinted in 2000

PHOTOGRAPHIC ACKNOWLEDGEMENTS
Abbreviations: NHIL – New Holland Image Library
Photographic positions: t = top, b = bottom, l = left, r = right
All photographs © Shaen Adey/NHIL except for the following:
Roger du Buisson: p. 6-7, 30-31; Jocelyn Burt: p. 116-117, 119; compliments of the Crown
Casino: p. 36; compliments of the Eureka Stockade Information Centre: p. 96, 97; Richard
l'Anson: 1/2 title, p. 12, 35, 41b, 61; Anthony Johnson/NHIL: p. 5, 11, 13, 22, 32r, 34,
54-55, 57; Melbourne Aquarium: p. 21; NHIL: p. 28, 118; compliments of the Phillip Island
Information Centre: p. 71b; Ron Ryan/Coo-ee Picture Library: p. 41t, 52, 104, 105; David
Simmonds: p. 9, 18, 19t&b, 20, 23, 24, 25, 26, 38, 40, 42-43, 50, 115;
compliments of the Tesselaar Tulip Farm: p. 63; Peter Walton: front cover

National Library of Australia Cataloguing-in-Publication Data:

Melbourne and Victoria's splendour.
ISBN 1 86436 373 8

1. Victoria – Pictorial works. 2. Melbourne (Vic.) – Pictorial works.

919.4500222

Publishing General Manager: Jane Hazell
Publisher: Averill Chase
Project Co-ordinator: Anna Sanders
Text written by: Emma Wise
Designer: DiZign Pty Ltd
Picture Researchers: Bronwyn Rennex and Raquel Hill
Reproduction by DNL Resources
Printed and bound in Malaysia by Times Offset (m) Sdn. Bhd.

Above: Farm sheds blend into parched paddocks at Yarck on the Maroondah Highway.

Previous pages: Storm clouds loom over the silvery waters of Lake Hume near Albury.